SON OF

FASTER

CHEAPER

SON OF FASTER CHEAPER

A Sharp Look Inside the Animation Business

Second Edition

Floyd Norman

THEME PARK PRESS

Editor: Bob McLain
Layout: Artisanal Text

ISBN 978-1-941500-37-8
Printed in the United States of America

Theme Park Press | www.ThemeParkPress.com
Address queries to bob@themeparkpress.com

Introduction

Other Books by Floyd Norman

Animated Life: A Lifetime of Tips, Tricks, Techniques, and Stories from an Animation Legend (2013)

Coming in 2015 from Theme Park Press

Faster Cheaper

Disk Drive

How the Grinch Stole Disney

Suspended Animation

A Crazy Business

Some years ago, an animation studio in the Los Angeles area suffered a major fire. Investigators speculated arson might be involved. A police detective scoffed at this notion. "Nonsense! Who would burn down a cartoon studio?" "Apparently," volunteered a disgruntled artist, "you've never worked in one."

This publishing experiment began nearly ten years ago when my first book, *Faster Cheaper*, rolled off the press. It consisted of funny sketches ripped off the wall of my cubicle. There's nothing profound here.

Just a bunch of gags about a crazy business.

Introduction

When I first arrived at the Disney studio in the late fifties, I remember all the funny gag drawings that lined the walls of G-wing in the Animation Building. The artists enjoyed the good-natured ribbing of each other, as well as of the studio management.

After the completion of *Sleeping Beauty*, the Animation Department went through a severe downsizing. Sadly, much of the humor also vanished. I hated to see a wonderful tradition come to a close, so I started drawing cartoons of my fellow artists, and of my boss, Walt Disney.

Over the years, I've become somewhat of an editorial cartoonist, as I chronicled the daily studio activities in the form of gag cartoons. I also kept a watchful eye on Walt Disney ruling over his kingdom. In the early 1980s, Michael Eisner brought new management to Disney, and in so doing, hundreds of new gag ideas.

I've drawn many, many cartoons at the Disney studio, Hanna-Barbera, and Pixar. Much to my surprise, I found that many artists had their own personal collections of my drawings. As an old gag cartoonist, I can't think of a better compliment.

CHAPTER ONE

Working for Walt

There's no comparison to the Disney Company of today and the studio the "Old Maestro" ran back in the fifties and sixties. Back then, it was a one-man show. Nothing, and I mean nothing, escaped Walt's careful gaze. When you said you worked for Walt Disney, you really meant it.

Though some executives feared his wrath, most of us dumb kids had nothing to fear. We were too unimportant to get into trouble. Walt Disney was a tough taskmaster, and you gave him nothing less than your best.

I enjoyed drawing gags about Walt. I would like to think he enjoyed them as well.

The old story guys always seemed to be reading newspapers and drinking coffee. I wondered when they got any work done. I doubt Walt ever said this, but it seemed like a funny idea.

Walt's famous scowl and tapping finger was real enough. Walter Miller, Disney's grandson, was pleased to show me he could mimic Walt's famous arched eyebrow.

TAP!
TAP! TAP!
TAP!
TAP!

Walt had a way of announcing his presence as he entered a wing of the Animation Building. Walt's cough, a loud "Harrrumph!" was a clear sign that "man was in the forest."

More often than not, the previous day's filming had gone badly. It was fun watching the movie executives squirm as they tried explaining this to Walt.

Early development on Winnie the Pooh was often a pain in the butt. There were times Walt considered giving the cute little bear the boot.

Whenever I saw Walt walk briskly out
of a story meeting, it was a pretty good
sign things had not gone well.

Back in the fifties, we had a visitor on the Disney lot who had worked as a missionary in Africa. This little "Church Lady" took issue with *The African Lion*, a Disney film recently produced. As luck would have it, my friend saw the Old Maestro walking past and introduced him to the missionary. Walt was very proud of the film, but the missionary pointed out all the inaccuracies. He was not pleased. We thought we would soon be out of a job.

"The blind leading the blind" pretty much sums up Disney's recent management.

As Walt's guys arrive at the Pearly Gates,
I'll bet they're catching it from their
boss for letting the studio go to hell.

Woolie Reithermann

CHAPTER TWO

The World of Bill and Joe

Long before The Cartoon Network, there was Hanna-Barbera, the landmark studio of Saturday morning cartoons. Back then, William Hanna and Joseph Barbera ruled Saturday morning and employed hundreds of animation artists.

Even though we dealt with tight schedules and tighter budgets, I can state for a fact that the artists came to work each morning with smiles on their faces. Try finding that today.

Okay, maybe the shows weren't all that funny, but I guarantee, the staff sure was.

NO MORE OVERSEAS PRODUCTION!
WE ARE SENDING ALL ANIMATION
TO ANOTHER PLANET!
TV

Hanna and Barbera even produced a series on the Bible. Members of the clergy were invited to supervise the scripts.

THE PRODUCER
NOBODY
COULD BEAT !

ROBERT DENIRO
AS

"RAGING BILL"

COMING SOON TO A
COUNTRY NEAR YOU

William Hanna's reputation as a tough manager was legendary.
In truth, he was one of the nicest men I ever knew.

"Hollywood Joe" and "Taskmaster Bill" were the subjects of endless cartoons. Many of the gags are now in the personal collections of former Hanna-Barbera artists.

CHAPTER THREE

The New Disney

I returned to the Disney studio in the 1980s, just in time to welcome the new management team of Michael Eisner and Frank Wells. Suddenly, sleepy little Disney found itself racing toward the Disney Decade, and the company would never be the same.

Yet, some things never change. This new team was a continual source of inspiration for new gags. A new breed of management had come to Disney, and I was ready for them.

Doing a riff on the popular *Frank and Ernest* gag panel, I
created my own weekly comic I called, *Frank and Eisner*.

Cash-strapped Disney was suddenly awash in money. Clearly, these new guys were miracle workers.

The new team never missed
a marketing opportunity.

I couldn't help but picture mountain climber
Frank Wells scaling the Animation Building.

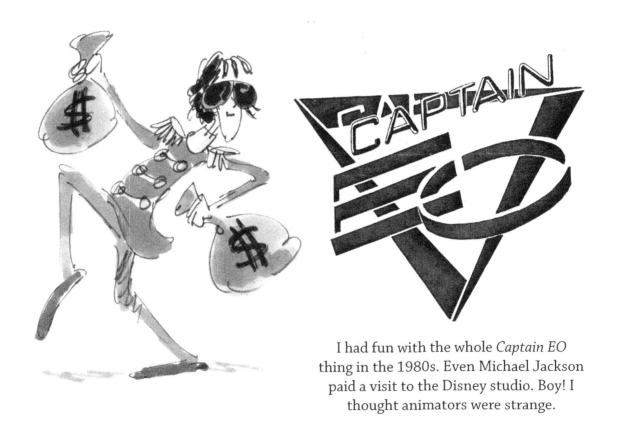

I had fun with the whole *Captain EO* thing in the 1980s. Even Michael Jackson paid a visit to the Disney studio. Boy! I thought animators were strange.

This is a reference to Jackson's hair catching on fire during a concert performance in 1984, and the publicity it spawned.

That's George Lucas and Francis Ford Coppola flanking
Jackson behind *Captain EO* film editor Walter Murch.

The early 1900s proved to be a tough time for Disney. The loss of Frank Wells and the departure of Jeffrey Katzenberg came as a shock to all. Then, it was announced that Eisner required heart surgery. Could things get any worse, we wondered? During this grim time, I felt a need to lighten things up.

And then there was the flirtation with the internet. Disney purchased go.com for millions and invested millions more. However, the only thing that seemed to "go" was the money.

CHAPTER FOUR

The Story Artist

Being a story artist is a crazy job. If the film is a hit, it's because of the gifted screenwriter or the talented director. If the film flops, it's probably the fault of the story artist.

Story artists make animated features work. Often the least acknowledged, they're the ones in the trenches pulling the film story together. The thankless job is often more pain than pleasure, but we do it anyway. Laughing at this job has always been the best way to deal with it.

There are times when we fail to please the director.

Screen credits on an animated film are usually posted for the crew to check out.
Yes, they're often just as bogus as their live-action counterparts.

CHAPTER FIVE

Animation Boom

I returned to Disney Animation in the 1990s, and found myself in a brave new world. Animators were now employed full time and earning good salaries. The animation boom was in full swing, and many thought it would go on forever. When this grizzled old animation veteran was offered a "signing bonus" for simply taking a job, I realized I had entered Animation Bizarro World.

The Lion King had earned a ton of money for Disney, so every studio in town wanted to hop on the animation gravy train. Sadly, the train was about to be derailed. Oh, for the good old days when animation was unprofitable, and a lot more fun.

Is your movie in trouble?
Maybe all you need is a title change.

I still love that Disney managed to keep this film "African free". Not one African was seen in the entire movie. When your story takes place in Africa, that takes some doing.

Think this is a dumb way to market a movie based on the Victor Hugo novel? Disney's marketing ideas were not that much better.

In *The Hunchback of Notre Dame*, Quasimodo is crowned the King of Fools. I would have made a different choice.

Actually, the movie has a happy ending. Too bad we can't say the same for Disney's Feature Animation Department.

Hunchback's opening did not meet
the studio's expectations. Truth is, the
executives at Disney had been spoiled.

SHE'S YOUNG. SHE'S BETROTHED. SHE'S PISSED.

WALT DISNEY
PICTURES PRESENTS

THE Legend OF MULAN

ONCE SHE
KICKS YOUR ASS,
AN HOUR LATER
SHE'LL KICK IT
AGAIN !

After my chores on *The Hunchback of Notre Dame*, I was sent to work on *Mulan*. After a rough start, this turned out to be a really terrific movie.

One of the great Disney heroines, this is one woman you don't want to mess with.

CHAPTER SIX

What I Really Want To Do Is, Direct

I've always believed in this rule: Anyone who wants to direct, probably shouldn't. There are always exceptions, but it probably isn't you.

Directing is not a job one should want. It's the damn job you get stuck with. I've watched young men grow old. I've seen full heads of hair turn gray overnight. I've listened to their bosses scream at them, and I've watched as they were carted off to the hospital a few days later. Such are the joys of helming a feature film.

I've worked with the best and the worst, but I love 'em all.

Directors get to work with annoying song writers. Oh, well, no job is perfect.

If we do our job well, this guy will leave animation
and take that live-action gig he's always wanted.

If the story doesn't work,
change the location.

It's not always the story that needs re-pinning.

CHAPTER SEVEN

To Insanity... And Beyond!

We've entered a new age of animation, when CEOs duke it out, technology encroaches, and animators ponder whether they've chosen the wrong career. Ironically, all this happens when animation is bigger than ever.

As always, though, animation will survive, and moronic executives will continue to provide me with plenty of gag material.

To insanity... and beyond!

Steve Jobs tells Eisner a thing or two, as John Lasseter looks on.

Steve Jobs is a hard sell,
even for Michael Eisner.

Traditional or digital, some things never change.

We can count on the press to come well-prepared.

Impressario

Launches brilliant
projects.

Broke studio owner. His
company went bust.

Maestro

Renowned for
artistic direction.

Animation director.
Can't find work because
he's too old.

Virtuoso

A master.

Veteran animator.
Unemployed.

back then...

just a few years later.

Animation had a new champion: Jeffrey
Katzenberg descended from the Mount.

It's always a special occasion when Eisner
visits your department.

During this incredible period, Disney Features ruled animation. Competitors appeared, but were continually slapped down by the eight-hundred-pound gorilla. I suppose it was only a matter of time before "beauty killed the beast".

Disney humor used to come out of character. Today, it comes out of another place.

Much to my surprise, I found out I would soon be retiring from the animation business. Since *Survivor* was a big hit on television, this seem to fit me perfectly.

After over 30 years, I walked out of
Disney one Friday afternoon. What the
hell. It was fun while it lasted.

Pirates of the Caribbean proved to be a big hit for
Disney. Ever wonder where the writers got the idea?

Oh, for the good old days
when executives were happy
to pick up a paycheck and stay
out of the creative process.

About the Author

Floyd Norman has worked in the animation business for over 50 years, so he knows where the "bodies are buried". His career as a story development artist spans from *The Jungle Book* with Walt Disney, to *Monsters, Inc.* at Pixar Animation Studios.

Never far from the animation industry either as a critic or consultant, Floyd now lives with his wife, Adrienne, in Pasadena and his home town of Santa Barbara. Floyd has five children and nine grandchildren.

So, you see, he didn't spend all his time drawing.

About the Publisher

Theme Park Press is the largest independent publisher of Disney and Disney-related pop culture books in the world.

Established in November 2012 by Bob McLain, Theme Park Press has released best-selling print and digital books about such topics as Disney films and animation, the Disney theme parks, Disney historical and cultural studies, park touring guides, autobiographies, fiction, and more.

For our complete catalog and a list of forthcoming titles, please visit:

ThemeParkPress.com

or contact the publisher at:

bob@themeparkpress.com

Theme Park Press Newsletter

For a free, occasional email newsletter to keep you posted on new book releases, new author signings, and other events, as well as contests and exclusive excerpts and supplemental content, send email to:

theband@themeparkpress.com

or sign up at

www.ThemeParkPress.com

More Books from Theme Park Press

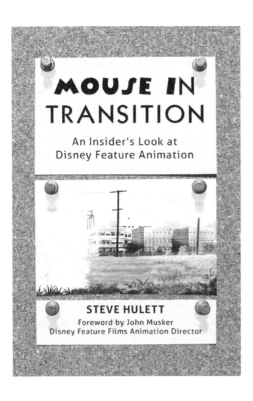

Mouse in Transition

An Insider's Look at
Disney Feature Animation

Steve Hulett's memoir of his decade
at the Disney Studio is a one-of-
a-kind chronicle of Disney's slow,
painful transition from the days
of Walt to the era of Eisner.

**ThemeParkPress.com/books/
mouse-transition.htm**

More Books from Theme Park Press

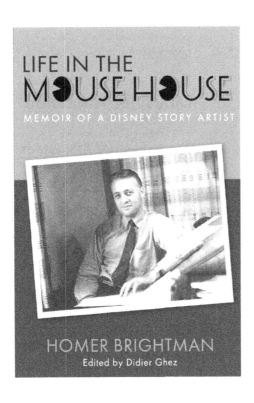

Life in the Mouse House

Homer Brightman's searing stories of working with Walt Disney and top Disney animators during the company's Golden Age.

Brightman recounts how Walt ruled the studio with fear, the endless posturing for Walt's favor, the studio's politically toxic culture, animator pranks and foibles, and more.

ThemeParkPress.com/books/ life-mouse-house.htm

More Books from Theme Park Press

More Books from Theme Park Press

Walt Disney and the Promise of Progress City

The Story of Walt's EPCOT

Disney historian and urban planner Sam Gennawey traces the evolution of the EPCOT we didn't get and the Epcot we did, in a tour-de-force analysis of Walt's vision for city-building and how his City of Tomorrow might have turned out had he lived.

ThemeParkPress.com/ books/progress-city.htm

Made in the USA
Middletown, DE
01 January 2021